POPE FRANCIS: WORDS OF MERCY AND JOY

Published 2013 by Veritas Publications
7–8 Lower Abbey Street, Dublin 1, Ireland
publications@veritas.ie
www.veritas.ie

ISBN 978 1 84730 541 1

A catalogue record for this book is available from the British
Library.

Designed by Lir Mac Cárthaigh, Veritas

Pope Francis cover photo: © CLAUDIO PERI/ANSA/Corbis.
Pope Francis arrives at the Chiesa Del Gesù in Rome on 31 July
2013. The Pontiff celebrates a Mass for St Ignatius of Loyola,
founder of the Society of Jesuits.

Printed in Ireland by SPRINT-print Ltd, Dublin

*Veritas books are printed on paper made from the wood pulp of
managed forests. For every tree felled, at least one tree is planted,
thereby renewing natural resources.*

POPE FRANCIS
Words of Mercy and Joy

VERITAS

⟫ Introduction ⟪

Since his election on 13 March 2013, Pope Francis is steadily proving himself to be one of the most popular and personable leaders on the world stage at the moment. Through his audiences, homilies and addresses, the Pope is showing himself to be a gifted speaker, conveying joy and thoughtfulness through simple language and relating to people with warmth and enthusiasm, through looks and through gestures. Coming across as someone both deep in wisdom and young at heart, the seventy-six-year-old pontiff's words are already reaching out to Catholics, non-Catholics, people of other faith and none, inspiring and rejuvenating many. Having embraced social media, the Pope has found connection with a whole new audience of people – the young in particular – and regularly tweets thought-provoking reflections on life and faith.

What follows are a select number of the Pope's words from various homilies and audiences, as well as some passages from interviews with *La Civiltà Cattolica* and *La Repubblica*, from the beginning of his apostolate to the end of the Year of Faith. The extracted passages give a sense, an essence, of the themes and topics important to our new Pope, Francis.

∽ On The Christian Life ∽

How does Joseph respond to his calling to be the protector of Mary, Jesus and the Church? By being constantly attentive to God, open to the signs of God's presence and receptive to God's plans, and not simply to his own. ... In him, dear friends, we learn how to respond to God's call, readily and willingly, but we also see the core of the Christian vocation, which is Christ! Let us protect Christ in our lives, so that we can protect others, so that we can protect creation! – *Inaugural Homily, March 19*

Being Christian is not just obeying orders but means being in Christ, thinking like him, acting like him, loving like him; it means letting him take possession of our life and change it, transform it, and free it from the darkness of evil and sin. ... Let us show the joy of being children of God, the freedom that living in Christ gives us which is true freedom, the freedom that saves us from the slavery of evil, of sin and of death! – *Audience, April 10*

We should all ask ourselves: How do I bear witness to Christ through my faith? Do I have the courage of Peter and the other Apostles, to think, to choose and to live as a Christian, obedient to God? To be sure, the testimony of faith comes in very many forms, just as in a great fresco, there is a variety of colours and shades; yet they are all important, even those which do not stand out ... There are the saints of every day, the 'hidden' saints, a sort of 'middle class of holiness', as a French author said, that 'middle class of holiness' to which we can all belong. But in different parts of the world, there are also those who suffer, like Peter and the Apostles, on account of the Gospel; there are those who give their lives in order to remain faithful to Christ by means of a witness marked by the shedding of their blood. Let us all remember this: one cannot proclaim the Gospel of Jesus without the tangible witness of one's life. Those who listen to us and observe us must be able to see in our actions what they hear from our lips, and so give glory to God! I am thinking now of some advice that Saint Francis of Assisi gave his brothers: preach the Gospel and, if necessary, use words. Preaching with your life, with your witness. Inconsistency on the part of pastors and the faithful between what they say and what they do, between word and manner of life, is undermining the Church's credibility. – *Homily, April 14*

TWEET! *A Christian is never bored or sad. Rather, the one who loves Christ is full of joy and radiates joy*

We too should be clear in our Christian life that entering the glory of God demands daily fidelity to his will, even when it demands sacrifice and sometimes requires us to change our plans. – *Audience, April 17*

In this period of crisis, today, it is important not to turn in on ourselves, burying our own talent, our spiritual, intellectual and material riches, everything that the Lord has given us, but rather to open ourselves, to be supportive, to be attentive to others. ... Set your stakes on great ideals, the ideals that enlarge the heart, the ideals of service that make your talents fruitful. Life is not given to us to be jealously guarded for ourselves, but is given to us so that we may give it in turn. – *Audience, April 24*

What is this joy? Is it to be happy? No, it is not the same. To be happy is good, yet joy is something more. It's another thing. It is something which does not depend on external motivations, or on passing issues: it is more profound. It is a gift. To be 'happy' at all moments at all cost, can at the end turn into superficiality and shallowness. This leaves us without Christian wisdom, which makes us dumb, naïve – right? All is joy ... no. Joy is something else; it is a gift from the Lord. – *Homily, May 10*

We are not Christian 'part-time', only at certain moments, in certain circumstances, in certain decisions; no one can be Christian in this way, we are Christian all the time! Totally! May Christ's truth, which the Holy Spirit teaches us and gives to us, always and totally affect our daily life. Let us call on him more often so that he may guide us on the path of disciples of Christ. Let us call on him every day. I am making this suggestion to you: let us invoke the Holy Spirit every day; in this way the Holy Spirit will bring us close to Jesus Christ. – *Audience, May 15*

For us Christians, wherever the Cross is, there is hope, always. If there is no hope, we are not Christian. That is why I like to say: do not allow yourselves to be robbed of hope. May we not be robbed of hope, because this strength is a grace, a gift from God which carries us forward with our eyes fixed on heaven. – *Homily, August 15*

❧ On Following Christ ❧

Ours is not a joy born of having many possessions, but from having encountered a Person, Jesus, in our midst; it is born from knowing that with him we are never alone, even at difficult moments, even when our life's journey comes up against problems and obstacles that seem insurmountable – and there are so many of them! And in this moment the enemy, the devil, comes, often disguised as an angel, and slyly speaks his word to us. Do not listen to him! Let us follow Jesus! – *Homily, March 24*

Following and accompanying Christ, staying with him, demands 'coming out of ourselves' … out of a dreary way of living faith that has become a habit, out of the temptation to withdraw into our own plans which end by shutting out God's creative action. – *Audience, March 27*

Christ opened the path to us. He is like a roped guide climbing a mountain who, on reaching the summit, pulls us up to him and leads us to God.

If we entrust our life to him, if we let ourselves be guided by him, we are certain to be in safe hands, in the hands of our Saviour, of our advocate. – *Audience, April 17*

An excellent programme for our lives: the Beatitudes and Matthew Chapter 25

On The Church

Let us ask ourselves today: how much do I love the Church? Do I pray for her? Do I feel part of the family of the Church? What do I do to ensure that she is a community in which each one feels welcome and understood, feels the mercy and love of God who renews life? Faith is a gift and an act which concern us personally, but God calls us to live with our faith together, as a family, as Church. – *Audience, May 29*

Dear brothers and sisters, let us ask God: help us to be members of the Body of the Church, ever more deeply united to Christ; help us not to cause the Body of the Church to suffer through our conflicts, our divisions, our selfishness. Help us to be living limbs bound one to the other by that unique force, love, which the Holy Spirit pours into our hearts (cf. Rm 5:5). – *Audience, June 19*

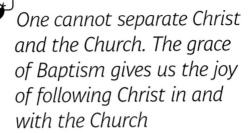

One cannot separate Christ and the Church. The grace of Baptism gives us the joy of following Christ in and with the Church

I would now like us to ask ourselves: how do we live our being Church? Are we living stones or are we, as it were, stones that are weary, bored or indifferent? Have you ever noticed how grim it is to see a tired, bored and indifferent Christian? A Christian like that is all wrong: the Christian must be alive, rejoicing in being Christian; he or she must live this beauty of belonging to the People of God which is the Church. Do we open ourselves to the action of the Holy Spirit, to be an active part of our communities, or do we withdraw into ourselves, saying; 'I have so much to do, it isn't my job'?

The Lord gives all of us his grace, his strength, so that we may be profoundly united to Christ, who is the cornerstone, the pillar and the foundation of our life and of the whole life of the Church. Let us pray that enlivened by his Spirit we may always be living stones of his Church. – *Audience, 26 June*

The image of the Church I like is that of the holy, faithful people of God. This is the definition I often use, and then there is that image from the Second Vatican Council's 'Dogmatic Constitution on the Church' (no. 12). Belonging to a people has a strong theological value. In the history of salvation, God has saved a people. There is no full identity without belonging to a people. No one is saved alone, as an isolated individual, but God attracts us looking at the complex web of relationships that take place in the human community. God enters into this dynamic, this participation in the web of human relationships. – La Civiltà Cattolica, *August 2013*

On The Church As
⤜ Mother ⤛

I dream of a Church that is a mother and shepherdess. – La Civiltà Cattolica, *August 2013*

The Church, like a good mother … accompanies our development by transmitting to us the Word of God, which is a light that directs the path of Christian life; she administers the Sacraments. She nourishes us with the Eucharist, she brings us the forgiveness of God through the Sacrament of Penance, she helps us in moments of sickness with the Anointing of the Sick. The Church accompanies us throughout our entire life of faith, throughout the whole of our Christian life. – *Audience, September 11*

[The Church] is a merciful mother who understands, who has always sought to help and encourage even those of her children who have erred or are erring; she never closes the door to home. She does not judge but offers God's forgiveness, she offers his love which invites even those of her children who have fallen into a deep abyss to continue on their way. The Church is not afraid to enter their darkness to give them hope; nor is the Church afraid to enter our darkness when we are in the dark night of our soul and our conscience to give us hope! Because the Church is mother! – *Audience, September 18*

On Evangelisation

To be sure, the testimony of faith comes in very many forms, just as in a great fresco, there is a variety of colours and shades, yet they are all important, even those which do not stand out. In God's great plan, every detail is important, even yours, even my humble little witness, even the hidden witness of those who live their faith with simplicity in everyday family relationships, work relationships, friendships. ... Let us all remember this: one cannot proclaim the Gospel of Jesus without the tangible witness of one's life. Those who listen to us and observe us must be able to see in our actions what they hear from our lips, and so give glory to God! – *Homily, April 14*

May you also be true evangelisers! May your initiatives be 'bridges', means of bringing others to Christ, so as to journey together with him. And in this spirit may you always be attentive to charity. Each individual Christian and every community is missionary to the extent that they bring to others and live the Gospel, and testify to God's love for all, especially those experiencing difficulties. – *Homily, May 5*

Evangelising is the Church's mission. It is not the mission of only a few, but it is mine, yours and our mission. The Apostle Paul exclaimed: 'Woe to me if I do not preach the Gospel!' (1 Cor 9:16). We must all be evangelisers, especially with our life! ...

We must all ask ourselves: how do I let myself be guided by the Holy Spirit in such a way that my life and my witness of faith is both unity and communion? Do I convey the word of reconciliation and of love, which is the Gospel, to the milieus in which I live? At times it seems that we are repeating today what happened at Babel: division, the incapacity to understand one another, rivalry, envy, egoism. What do I do with my life? Do I create unity around me? Or do I cause division, by gossip, criticism or envy? ...

Spreading the Gospel means that we are the first to proclaim and live the reconciliation, forgiveness, peace, unity and love which the Holy Spirit gives us. Let us remember Jesus' words: 'By this all men will know that you are my disciples, if you have love for one another' (Jn 13: 34-35). – *Audience, May 22*

Jesus sends his followers out with no 'purse, no bag, no sandals' (Lk 10:4). The spread of the Gospel is not guaranteed either by the number of persons, or by the prestige of the institution, or by the quantity of available resources. What counts is to be permeated by the love of Christ, to let oneself be led by the Holy Spirit and to graft one's own life onto the tree of life, which is the Lord's Cross. – *Homily, July 7*

On Ministry And
Service

God thinks like the Samaritan who did not pass by the unfortunate man, pitying him or looking at him from the other side of the road, but helped him without asking for anything in return; without asking whether he was a Jew, a pagan or a Samaritan, whether he was rich or poor. He asked for nothing. He went to help him. God is like this. — *Audience, March 27*

This I ask you; be shepherds, with the 'odour of the sheep', make it real, as shepherds among your flock, fishers of men. ... Dear priests, may our people sense that we are the Lord's disciples; may they feel that their names are written upon our priestly vestments and that we seek no other identity; and may they receive through our words and deeds the oil of gladness which Jesus, the anointed one, came to bring us. — *Homily, Chrism Mass, March 28*

Help one another: This is what Jesus teaches us, and this is what I am doing – and doing with all my heart – because it is my duty. As a priest and a bishop, I must be at your service. But it is a duty that comes from my heart. I love it. – *Homily, Mass of the Lord's Supper, March 28*

So, as I look out at you, I think: Who are catechists? They are people who keep the memory of God alive; they keep it alive in themselves and they are able to revive it in others. This is something beautiful: to remember God ... faith contains our own memory of God's history with us, the memory of our encountering God who always takes the first step, who creates, saves and transforms us. Faith is remembrance of his word which warms our heart, and of his saving work which gives life, purifies us, cares for and nourishes us. A catechist is a Christian who puts this remembrance at the service of proclamation, not to seem important, not to talk about himself or herself, but to talk about God, about his love and his fidelity. To talk about and to pass down all that God has revealed, his teaching in its totality, neither trimming it down nor adding on to it … Catechists are men and women of the memory of God if they have a constant, living relationship with him and with their neighbour; if they are men and women of faith who truly trust in God and put their security in him; if they are men and women of charity, love, who see others as brothers and sisters; if they are men and women of *hypomoné*, endurance and perseverance, able to face difficulties, trials and failures with serenity and hope in the Lord; if they are gentle, capable of understanding and mercy. – *Homily, September 29*

On Grace And
Forgiveness

The Lord never tires of forgiving – never! It is we who tire of asking his forgiveness. Let us ask for the grace not to tire of asking for forgiveness, because he never tires of forgiving. Let us ask for this grace. – *Homily, March 17*

Sometimes it may seem as though God does not react to evil, as if he is silent. And yet God has spoken. He has replied, and his answer is the cross of Christ: a word that is love, mercy, forgiveness. – *Address, Good Friday, March 29*

TWEET!

God's forgiveness is stronger than any sin

This is the invitation which I address to everyone: Let us accept the grace of Christ's resurrection! Let us be renewed by God's mercy; let us be loved by Jesus; let us enable the power of his love to transform our lives, too; and let us become agents of this mercy, channels through which God can water the earth, protect all creation and make justice and peace flourish. – Urbi et Orbi *Message, Easter Sunday, March 31*

You could say to me: but the Church is made up of sinners, we see them everyday. And this is true: we are a Church of sinners; and we sinners are called to let ourselves be transformed, renewed, sanctified by God. There has been in history the temptation for some to say: the Church is only the Church of the pure, the perfectly consistent, and expels all the rest. This is not true! This is heresy! The Church, that is holy, does not reject sinners; she does not reject us all; she does not reject because she calls everyone, welcomes them, is open even to those furthest from her, she calls everyone to allow themselves to be enfolded by the mercy, the tenderness and the forgiveness of the Father, who offers everyone the possibility of meeting him, of journeying toward sanctity. – *Audience, October 2*

On Courage And Mercy

We must not be afraid of being Christian and living as Christians! We must have this courage to go and proclaim the Risen Christ, for he is our peace; he made peace with his love, with his forgiveness, with his blood and with his mercy. – Regina Caeli, *April 7*

Pay attention, my young friends: to go against the current, this is good for the heart, but we need courage to swim against the tide. … We Christians were not chosen by the Lord for little things; push onwards toward the highest principles. Stake your lives on noble ideals, my dear young people! – *Homily, April 28*

What does freedom mean? It is certainly not doing whatever you want, allowing yourself to be dominated by the passions, to pass from one experience to another without discernment, to follow the fashions of the day; freedom does not mean, so to speak, throwing everything that you don't like out the window. … Let us not be afraid of life commitments, commitments that take up and concern our entire life! In this way our life will be fruitful! And this is freedom: to have the courage to make these decisions with generosity. – *Address, May 4*

I believe this is the time of mercy. This change of epoch, also because of many problems of the Church – such as the example of some priests who aren't good, also the problems of corruption in the Church and also the problem of clericalism, for example – has left many wounds, many wounds. The Church is a mother: It must reach out to heal the wounds, yes? With mercy. It must find mercy for everyone, no? I think about how when the Prodigal Son returned home, his father didn't say: 'But you, listen, sit down. What did you do with the money?' No, he held a party. Then, maybe, when the son wanted to talk, he talked. The Church must do the same. ... but, it's not enough to wait for them: we must go and seek them. This is mercy. And I believe that is a *kairos*: this time is a *kairos* of mercy. – *in conversation with journalists, July 28*

On The Truth Of Being
Human

Before all else, we need to keep alive in our world the thirst for the absolute, and to counter the dominance of a one-dimensional vision of the human person, a vision that reduces human beings to what they produce and to what they consume. This is one of the most insidious temptations of our time. – *Address, March 20*

Francis of Assisi tells us we should work to build peace. But there is no true peace without truth! There cannot be true peace if everyone is his own criterion, if everyone can always claim exclusively his own rights, without at the same time caring for the good of others, of everyone, on the basis of the nature that unites every human being on this earth. – *Address, March 22*

Man is like a traveller who, crossing the deserts of life, thirsts for the living water: gushing and fresh, capable of quenching his deep desire for light, love, beauty and peace. We all feel this desire! And Jesus gives us this living water; he is the Holy Spirit, who proceeds from the Father and whom Jesus pours out into our hearts. — *Audience, May 8*

On Family Life

Today the Church celebrates the parents of the Virgin Mary, the grandparents of Jesus, Saints Joachim and Anne. In their home, Mary came into the world, accompanied by the extraordinary mystery of the Immaculate Conception. Mary grew up in the home of Joachim and Anne; she was surrounded by their love and faith: in their home she learned to listen to the Lord and to follow his will. Saints Joachim and Anne were part of a long chain of people who had transmitted their love for God, expressed in the warmth and love of family life, down to Mary, who received the Son of God in her womb and who gave him to the world, to us. How precious is the family as the privileged place for transmitting the faith! ... – *Angelus, July 26*

Argue as much as you want; if the plates start flying, so be it. But never let the day end without making peace. Never! – *Homily, October 4*

How often do we say 'thank you' to one another in our families? These are essential words for our life in common. 'Sorry', 'excuse me', 'thank you'. If families can say these three things, they will be fine. – *Homily, October 20*

Dear families, you know very well that the true joy which we experience in the family is not superficial; it does not come from material objects, from the fact that everything seems to be going well … True joy comes from a profound harmony between persons, something which we all feel in our hearts and which makes us experience the beauty of togetherness, of mutual support along life's journey. But the basis of this feeling of deep joy is the presence of God, the presence of God in the family and his love, which is welcoming, merciful, and respectful towards all. … Dear families, always live in faith and simplicity, like the Holy Family of Nazareth! – *Homily, October 27*

On Prayer And The
❧ Family ❧

In this month of May, I would like to recall the importance and beauty of the prayer of the Holy Rosary. Reciting the Hail Mary, we are led to contemplate the mysteries of Jesus, that is, to reflect on the key moments of his life, so that, as with Mary and St Joseph, he is the centre of our thoughts, of our attention and our actions. It would be nice if, especially in this month of May, we could pray the Holy Rosary together in the family, with friends, in the parish, or [make] some prayer to Jesus and the Virgin Mary. Praying together is a precious moment that further strengthens family life and friendship. Let us learn to pray more in the family and as a family! – *Audience, May 1*

First: the family prays. … I would like to ask you, dear families: do you pray together from time to time as a family? … Praying the Our Father together, around the table, is not something extraordinary: it's easy. And praying the Rosary together, as a family, is very beautiful and a source of great strength. And also praying for one another! The husband for his wife, the wife for her husband, both together for their children, the children for their grandparents ... praying for each other. This is what it means to pray in the family and it is what makes the family strong: prayer. – *Homily, October 27*

On Young People

To listen to the Lord, we must learn to contemplate, feel his constant presence in our lives and we must stop and converse with him, give him space in prayer. Each of us, even you boys and girls, young people, so many of you here this morning, should ask yourselves: 'How much space do I give to the Lord? Do I stop to talk with him?' Ever since we were children, our parents have taught us to start and end the day with a prayer, to teach us to feel that the friendship and the love of God accompanies us. Let us remember the Lord more in our daily life! – *Audience, May 1*

TWEET!

Dear young people, do not bury your talents, the gifts that God has given you! Do not be afraid to dream of great things

Let us encourage the generosity which is typical of the young and help them to work actively in building a better world. Young people are a powerful engine for the Church and for society. They do not need material things alone; also and above all, they need to have held up to them those non-material values which are the spiritual heart of a people, the memory of a people. – *Homily, July 24*

Dear young friends, as you return to your homes, do not be afraid to be generous with Christ, to bear witness to his Gospel. ... Bringing the Gospel is bringing God's power to pluck up and break down evil and violence, to destroy and overthrow the barriers of selfishness, intolerance and hatred, so as to build a new world. Dear young friends, Jesus Christ is counting on you! The Church is counting on you! The Pope is counting on you! – *Homily on the Occasion of the 28th World Youth Day, July 28*

On The Environment And
Care For Creation

Please, I would like to ask all those who have positions of responsibility in economic, political and social life, and all men and women of goodwill: let us be 'protectors' of creation, protectors of God's plan inscribed in nature, protectors of one another and of the environment. Let us not allow omens of destruction and death to accompany the advance of this world! But to be 'protectors', we also have to keep watch over ourselves! Let us not forget that hatred, envy and pride defile our lives! ...

To protect creation, to protect every man and every woman, to look upon them with tenderness and love, is to open up a horizon of hope; it is to let a shaft of light break through the heavy clouds; it is to bring the warmth of hope! For believers, for us Christians, like Abraham, like Saint Joseph, the hope that we bring is set against the horizon of God, which has opened up before us in Christ. It is a hope built on the rock which is God. – *Homily, March 19*

So this is the invitation which I address to everyone: Let us accept the grace of Christ's Resurrection! Let us be renewed by God's mercy, let us be loved by Jesus, let us enable the power of his love to transform our lives too; and let us become agents of this mercy, channels through which God can water the earth, protect all creation and make justice and peace flourish. Peace to the whole world, torn apart by violence linked to drug trafficking and by the iniquitous exploitation of natural resources! Peace to this our Earth! May the risen Jesus bring comfort to the victims of natural disasters and make us responsible guardians of creation. – *Homily, March 31*

Take good care of creation. Saint Francis wanted that. People occasionally forgive, but nature never does. If we don't take care of the environment, there's no way of getting around it. – *Meeting with the President of Ecuador, April 22*

TWEET!

Let us keep a place for Christ in our lives, let us care for one another and let us be loving custodians of creation

There was a time when our grandparents were very careful not to throw away any leftover food. Consumerism has induced us to be accustomed to excess and to the daily waste of food, whose value, which goes far beyond mere financial parameters, we are no longer able to judge correctly. Let us remember well, however, that whenever food is thrown out it is as if it were stolen from the table of the poor, from the hungry! I ask everyone to reflect on the problem of the loss and waste of food, to identify ways and approaches which, by seriously dealing with this problem, convey solidarity and sharing with the underprivileged. – *Audience, June 5*

39

On The 'People Of God'

What does 'People of God' mean? First of all it means that God does not belong in a special way to any one people; for it is he who calls us, convokes us, invites us to be part of his people, and this invitation is addressed to all, without distinction, for the mercy of God 'desires all men to be saved' (1 Tm 2:4). Jesus does not tell the Apostles or us to form an exclusive group, a group of the elite. Jesus says: go out and make disciples of all people (cf. Mt 28:19). Saint Paul says that in the People of God, in the Church, 'there is neither Jew nor Greek … for you are all one in Christ Jesus' (Gal 3:28). I would also like to say to anyone who feels far away from God and the Church, to anyone who is timid or indifferent, to those who think they can no longer change: the Lord calls you too to become part of his people and he does this with great respect and love! He invites us to be part of this people, the People of God! – *Audience, June 12*

I would like to tell those who feel indifferent to God, to faith, and those who are far from God or who have distanced themselves from him, [and us] too, with our 'distancing' and our 'abandonment' of God, that may seem insignificant but are so numerous in our daily life: look into the depths of your heart, look into your own inner depths and ask yourself: do you have a heart that desires something great, or a heart that has been lulled to sleep by things? Has your heart preserved the restlessness of seeking or have you let it be suffocated by things that end by hardening it? God awaits you, he seeks you; how do you respond to him? Are you aware of the situation of your soul? Or have you nodded off? Do you believe God is waiting for you or does this truth consist only of 'words'? – *Homily, August 28*

On Mary As A Model Of
⚫ Faith ⚫

Mary … the Mother of Christ and of the Church is always with us. She walks with us always, she is with us. … She has of course already entered, once and for all, into heavenly glory. But this does not mean that she is distant or detached from us; rather Mary accompanies us, struggles with us, sustains Christians in their fight against the forces of evil. – *Homily, August 15*

After the Annunciation, [Mary's] first act is one of charity towards her elderly kinswoman Elizabeth. Her first words are: 'My soul magnifies the Lord', in other words, a song of praise and thanksgiving to God not only for what he did for her, but for what he had done throughout the history of salvation. Everything is his gift. If we can realise that everything is God's gift, how happy will our hearts be! – *Homily, October 13*

How did Mary live [her] faith? She lived it out in the simplicity of the thousand daily tasks and worries of every mother, such as providing food, clothing, caring for the house … It was precisely Our Lady's normal life which served as the basis for the unique relationship and profound dialogue which unfolded between her and God, between her and her Son. Mary's 'yes', already perfect from the start, grew until the hour of the Cross. There her motherhood opened to embrace every one of us, our lives, so as to guide us to her Son. Mary lived perpetually immersed in the mystery of God-made-man, as his first and perfect disciple, by contemplating all things in her heart in the light of the Holy Spirit, in order to understand and live out the will of God. – *Audience, October 23*

On Peace And Caring For
～ Others ～

'Where is your brother? Who is responsible for this blood?' In Spanish literature we have a comedy of Lope de Vega which tells how the people of the town of Fuente Ovejuna kill their governor because he is a tyrant. They do it in such a way that no one knows who the actual killer is. So when the royal judge asks: 'Who killed the governor?' they all reply: 'Fuente Ovejuna, sir'. Everybody and nobody! Today too, the question has to be asked: Who is responsible for the blood of these brothers and sisters of ours? Nobody! That is our answer: It isn't me; I don't have anything to do with it; it must be someone else, but certainly not me. Yet God is asking each of us: 'Where is the blood of your brother which cries out to me?' Today no one in our world feels responsible; we have lost a sense of responsibility for our brothers and sisters. We have fallen into the hypocrisy of the priest and the levite whom Jesus described in the parable of the Good Samaritan: we see our brother half dead on the side of the road, and perhaps we say to ourselves: 'poor soul …!', and then go on our way. It's not our responsibility, and with that we feel reassured, assuaged. The culture of comfort, which makes us think only of ourselves, makes us insensitive to the cries of other people, makes us live in soap bubbles which, however lovely, are insubstantial; they offer a fleeting and empty illusion which results in indifference to others; indeed, it even leads to the globalisation of indifference. In this globalised world, we have fallen into globalised indifference. We have become used to the suffering of others: it doesn't affect me; it doesn't concern me; it's none of my business! … Lord, in this liturgy, a penitential liturgy, we beg forgiveness for our indifference to so many of our brothers and sisters. Father, we ask your pardon for those who are complacent and closed amid comforts which have deadened their hearts; we beg your forgiveness for those who by their decisions on the global level have created situations that lead to these tragedies. Forgive us, Lord! – *Homily, July 8*

How I wish that all men and women of good will would look to the Cross if only for a moment! There, we can see God's reply: violence is not answered with violence, death is not answered with the language of death. In the silence of the Cross, the uproar of weapons ceases and the language of reconciliation, forgiveness, dialogue and peace is spoken. This evening, I ask the Lord that we Christians, and our brothers and sisters of other religions, and every man and woman of good will, cry out forcefully: violence and war are never the way to peace! Let everyone be moved to look into the depths of his or her conscience and listen to that word which says: Leave behind the self-interest that hardens your heart, overcome the indifference that makes your heart insensitive towards others, conquer your deadly reasoning, and open yourself to dialogue and reconciliation. – *Homily, September 7*

On The Mass, Prayer And The Sacraments

Mass is an encounter with Jesus, not a 'social event'. Every week we go to church, or rather when someone dies, we go to the funeral … and this memory oftentimes bores us, because it is not near. It is sad, but the Mass is often turned into a social event and we are not close to the memory of the Church, which is the presence of the Lord before us. Imagine this beautiful scene in the Book of Nehemiah: Ezra who carries the Book of Israel's memory and the people once again grow near to their memory and weep, the heart is warmed, is joyful, it feels that the joy of the Lord is its strength – and the people makes a feast, without fear, simply. – *Homily, March 10*

No, you cannot pray with enemies in your heart, with brothers and enemies in your heart, you cannot pray. This is difficult, yes; it is difficult, not easy. 'I cannot say "Father", I cannot … I cannot say "Our", because he did this to me and this …

I cannot! They must go to hell, right? I will have nothing to do with them.' It's true, it is not easy. But Jesus has promised us the Holy Spirit: it is he who teaches us, from within, from the heart, how to say 'Father' and how to say 'Our'. Today we ask the Holy Spirit to teach us to say 'Father' and to be able to say 'Our', and thus make peace with all our enemies. – *Homily, June 20*

TWEET!

Our prayer cannot be reduced to an hour on Sundays. It is important to have a daily relationship with the Lord

The Angelus prayer is a beautiful popular expression of the faith. It is a simple prayer, recited at three specific times during the day. It thus punctuates the rhythm of our daily activities: in the morning, at midday, and at sunset. But it is an important prayer. I encourage each of you to recite it, along with the Hail Mary. It reminds us of a luminous event which transformed history: the Incarnation, the moment when the Son of God became man in Jesus of Nazareth. – *Angelus, July 26*

 If we are to know the Lord, we must go to him. Listen to him in silence before the tabernacle and approach him in the Sacraments

The Sacrament is not a magic rite: it is an encounter with Jesus Christ; we encounter the Lord – it is he who is beside us and accompanies us. – *Homily, September 24*

﹏ On The Holy Spirit ﹏

We should get into the habit of asking ourselves, before the end of the day: 'What did the Holy Spirit do in me? What witness did he give me?' Because he is a divine presence that helps us [in] moving forward in our lives as Christians. – *Homily, May 6*

Let us allow ourselves to be guided by the Holy Spirit, let us allow him to speak to our heart and say this to us: God is love, God is waiting for us, God is Father, he loves us as a true father loves, he loves us truly and only the Holy Spirit can tell us this in our hearts. Let us hear the Holy Spirit, let us listen to the Holy Spirit, and may we move forward on this path of love, mercy and forgiveness. – *Audience, May 8*

This is a prayer we must pray every day: 'Holy Spirit, make my heart open to the word of God, make my heart open to goodness, make my heart open to the beauty of God every day.' I would like to ask everyone a question: how many of you pray every day to the Holy Spirit? There will not be many but we must fulfil Jesus' wish and pray every day to the Holy Spirit that he open our heart to Jesus … We need to let ourselves be bathed in the light of the Holy Spirit so that he may lead us into the Truth of God, who is the one Lord of our life. … May Christ's truth, which the Holy Spirit teaches us and gives to us, always and totally affect our daily life. Let us call on him more often so that he may guide us on the path of disciples of Christ. Let us call on him every day. I am making this suggestion to you: let us invoke the Holy Spirit every day, in this way the Holy Spirit will bring us close to Jesus Christ. – *Audience, May 15*

On Religious Life

Dear Brothers, let's show courage. Half of us are in our golden years. But old age is the source of wisdom. Elders carry the wisdom that comes with life. It reminds me of Simeon and Anna in the Temple, who because of their age were able to recognise Jesus clearly. Let's pass on this wisdom to the young. Just like good wine improves with time, so does wisdom. Let's pass this on to other generations. – *Address to Cardinals, March 15*

Dear priests, may God the Father renew in us the Spirit of holiness with whom we have been anointed. May he renew his Spirit in our hearts, that this anointing may spread to everyone, even to those 'outskirts' where our faithful people most look for it and most appreciate it. – *Homily, March 28*

Remember then that you are taken from among men and appointed on their behalf for those things that pertain to God. Therefore, carry out the ministry of Christ the Priest with constant joy and genuine love, attending not to your own concerns but to those of Jesus Christ. You are pastors, not functionaries. Be mediators, not intermediaries. – *Homily, April 21*

Jesus, at the Last Supper, turns to the Apostles with these words: 'You did not choose me, but I chose you' (Jn 15:16). They remind us all, not only us who are priests, that vocation is always an initiative of God. It is Christ who called you to follow him in the consecrated life and this means continuously making an 'exodus' from yourselves in order to centre your life on Christ and on his Gospel, on the will of God, laying aside your own plans, in order to say with St Paul: 'It is no longer I who live, but Christ who lives in me' (Gal 2:20). – *Address to Heads of Women's Religious Communities, May 8*

On Women In The
Church

It is necessary to broaden the opportunities for a stronger presence of women in the Church. I am wary of a solution that can be reduced to a kind of 'female machismo', because a woman has a different make-up than a man. But what I hear about the role of women is often inspired by an ideology of machismo ... The Church cannot be herself without the woman and her role. The woman is essential for the Church. Mary, a woman, is more important than the bishops. I say this because we must not confuse the function with the dignity. We must therefore investigate further the role of women in the Church. We have to work harder to develop a profound theology of the woman. Only by making this step will it be possible to better reflect on their function within the Church ... The challenge today is this: to think about the specific place of women also in those places where the authority of the Church is exercised for various areas of the Church.
– La Civiltà Cattolica, *August 2013*

On His Pontificate

Today, together with the feast of Saint Joseph, we are celebrating the beginning of the ministry of the new Bishop of Rome, the Successor of Peter, which also involves a certain power. Certainly, Jesus Christ conferred power upon Peter, but what sort of power was it? Jesus' three questions to Peter about love are followed by three commands: feed my lambs, [tend my sheep], feed my sheep.

… Let us never forget that authentic power is service, and that the Pope too, when exercising power, must enter ever more fully into that service which has its radiant culmination on the Cross. He must be inspired by the lowly, concrete and faithful service which marked Saint Joseph and, like him, he must open his arms to protect all of God's people and embrace with tender affection the whole of humanity, especially the poorest, the weakest, the least important, those whom Matthew lists in the final judgment on love: the hungry, the thirsty, the stranger, the naked, the sick and those in prison (cf. Mt 25:31-46). Only those who serve with love are able to protect! – *Inaugural Homily, March 19*

Discernment is one of the things that worked inside St Ignatius. For him it is an instrument of struggle in order to know the Lord and follow him more closely. ... This discernment takes time. For example, many think that changes and reforms can take place in a short time. I believe that we always need time to lay the foundations for real, effective change. And this is the time of discernment. Sometimes discernment instead urges us to do precisely what you had at first thought you would do later. And that is what has happened to me in recent months. Discernment is always done in the presence of the Lord, looking at the signs, listening to the things that happen, the feeling of the people, especially the poor. My choices, including those related to the day-to-day aspects of life, like the use of a modest car, are related to a spiritual discernment that responds to a need that arises from looking at things, at people, and from reading the signs of the times. Discernment in

the Lord guides me in my way of governing. – La
Civiltà Cattolica, *August 2013*

TWEET! *True power is service. The
Pope must serve all people,
especially the poor, the
weak, the vulnerable*

Before I accepted, I asked if I could spend a few
minutes in the room next to the one with the
balcony overlooking the square. My head was
completely empty and I was seized by a great
anxiety. To make it go away and relax, I closed
my eyes and made every thought disappear, even
the thought of refusing to accept the position, as
the liturgical procedure allows. I closed my eyes
and I no longer had any anxiety or emotion. At
a certain point I was filled with a great light. It
lasted a moment, but to me it seemed very long.
Then the light faded, I got up suddenly and walked
into the room where the cardinals were waiting and

the table on which was the act of acceptance. – La Repubblica, *October 2013*

I'm not Francis of Assisi and I do not have his strength and his holiness. But I am the Bishop of Rome and Pope of the Catholic world. The first thing I decided was to appoint a group of eight cardinals to be my advisers. Not courtiers but wise people who share my own feelings. This is the beginning of a Church with an organisation that is not just top-down but also horizontal. When Cardinal Martini talked about focusing on the councils and synods he knew how long and difficult it would be to go in that direction. Gently, but firmly and tenaciously. – La Repubblica, *October 2013*

On How The Pope
⟫⟫⟫ Prays ⟪⟪⟪

I pray the Breviary every morning. I like to pray with the psalms. Then, later, I celebrate Mass. I pray the Rosary. What I really prefer is adoration in the evening, even when I get distracted and think of other things, or even fall asleep praying. In the evening then, between seven and eight o'clock, I stay in front of the Blessed Sacrament for an hour in adoration. But I pray mentally even when I am waiting at the dentist or at other times of the day.

Prayer for me is always a prayer full of memory, of recollection, even the memory of my own history or what the Lord has done in his Church or in a particular parish. For me it is the memory of which St Ignatius speaks in the First Week of the Exercises in the encounter with the merciful Christ crucified. And I ask myself: 'What have I done for Christ? What am I doing for Christ? What should I do for Christ?' It is the memory of which Ignatius speaks in the 'Contemplation for Experiencing Divine Love,' when he asks us to recall the gifts we have received. But above all, I also know that the Lord remembers me. I can forget about him, but I know that he never, ever forgets me. Memory has a fundamental role for the heart of a Jesuit: memory of grace, the memory mentioned in Deuteronomy, the memory of God's works that are the basis of the covenant between God and the people. It is this memory that makes me his son and that makes me a father, too. – La Civiltà Cattolica, *August 2013*

The key that opens the door to the faith is prayer … When a Christian prays, he is not far from the faith; he speaks with Jesus … I say to pray, I do not say to say prayers … It is one thing to pray, and another thing to say prayers. – *Homily, October 17*

On Jorge Mario
～ Bergoglio ～

I do not know what might be the most fitting description [of myself] … I am a sinner. This is the most accurate definition. It is not a figure of speech, a literary genre. I am a sinner. … Yes, perhaps I can say that I am a bit astute, that I can adapt to circumstances, but it is also true that I am a bit naïve. But the best summary, the one that comes more from the inside and I feel most true is this: I am a sinner whom the Lord has looked upon. I am one who is looked upon by the Lord. I always felt my motto, *Miserando atque Eligendo* [By Having Mercy and By Choosing Him], was very true for me. – La Civiltà Cattolica, *August 2013*

My style of government as a Jesuit at the beginning had many faults. That was a difficult time for the Society: an entire generation of Jesuits had disappeared. Because of this I found myself provincial when I was still very young. I was only thirty-six years old. That was crazy. I had to deal with difficult situations, and I made my decisions abruptly and by myself. Yes, but I must add one thing: when I entrust something to someone, I totally trust that person. He or she must make a really big mistake before I rebuke that person. But despite this, eventually people get tired of authoritarianism … My authoritarian and quick manner of making decisions led me to have serious problems and to be accused of being ultraconservative. I lived a time of great interior crisis when I was in Cordova. To be sure, I have never been like Blessed Imelda [thought to be incorrupt], but I have never been a right-winger. It was my authoritarian way of making decisions that created problems … I say these things from life experience and because I want to make clear what the dangers are. Over time I learned many things. The Lord has allowed this growth in knowledge of government through my faults and my sins. So as Archbishop of Buenos Aires, I had a meeting with the six auxiliary bishops every two weeks, and several times a year with the council of priests. They asked questions and we opened the floor for discussion. This greatly helped me to make the best decisions. But now I hear some people tell me: 'Do not consult too much, and decide by yourself.' Instead, I believe that consultation is very important. – La Civiltà Cattolica, *August 2013*

And then a thing that is really important for me: community. I was always looking for a community. I did not see myself as a priest on my own. I need a community. And you can tell this by the fact that I am here in Santa Marta. At the time of the conclave I lived in Room 207. (The rooms were assigned by drawing lots.) This room where we are now was a guest room. I chose to live here, in Room 201, because when I took possession of the papal apartment, inside myself I distinctly heard a 'no.' The papal apartment in the Apostolic Palace is not luxurious. It is old, tastefully decorated and large, but not luxurious. But in the end it is like an inverted funnel. It is big and spacious, but the entrance is really tight. People can come only in dribs and drabs, and I cannot live without people. I need to live my life with others. – La Civiltà Cattolica, *August 2013*

All homily, audience and address passages taken from www.vatican.va; passages also taken from La Civiltà Cattolica, *August 2013, from an interview with Antonio Spadaro, SJ, editor in chief: http://www.americamagazine.org/pope-interview; and from* La Repubblica, *October 2013, from an interview with Eugenio Scalfari, founder of the newspaper: http://www.repubblica.it/cultura/2013/10/01/news/pope_s_conversation_with_scalfari_english-67643118/. Visit these websites to find many more of the words to date of Pope Francis.*